# This ONE Thing:

# The Plan, The Priority, The Promise of His Presence

# This ONE Thing

The Plan, The Priority, The Promise of His Presence

## CHARITY MORRIS

*This ONE Thing*
The Plan, The Priority, The Promise of His Presence

Charity A. Morris

Copyright © 2019 by Charity A. Morris

Published by Scribe Publications
404-919-1931
http://www.scribepublicationsinc.com

Cover Art and Design by Corey Scott

All rights reserved. This book or parts thereof may not be reproduced in any form, stored in a retrieval system, or transmitted in any form by any means - electronic, mechanical, photocopy, recording, or otherwise - without prior written permission of the publisher, except as provided by United States of America copyright law.

Unless otherwise identified, scripture quotations are from the Holy Bible King James Version, Cambridge, 1769. Used by permission. All rights reserved.

Scripture quotations marked AMP are taken from the Amplified Bible, Copyright (c) 1954, 1958, 1962, 1964, 1965, 1987 by The Lockman Foundation. Used by permission. (www.Lockman.org).

Scripture quotations noted NLT are from the Holy Bible, New Living Translation. Copyright (c) 1996 and 2004. Used by permission of Tyndale House Publishers, Wheaton, Illinois. 60190. All rights reserved.

Scripture quotations noted MSG are from the *The Message*. Copyright © 1993, 1994, 1995, 1996, 2000, 2001, 2002. Used by permission of NavPress Publishing Group.

Scripture quotations noted TLB are from The Living Bible copyright © 1971 by Tyndale House Foundation. Used by permission of Tyndale House Publishers Inc., Carol Stream, Illinois 60188. All rights reserved.

Scripture quotations noted (ESV) are from The ESV® Bible (The Holy Bible, English Standard Version®) copyright © 2001 by Crossway, a publishing ministry of Good News Publishers. ESV® Text Edition: 2011. The ESV® text has been reproduced in cooperation with and by permission of Good News Publishers.

Any name referencing satan will not be given the respect of capitalization, even at the risk of improper sentence structure.

ISBN-13: 978-0-9967824-4-9

Library of Congress Control Number: 2019906399

Printed in the United States of America.

## Dedication

This book is dedicated to all who are seeking a greater level of intimacy with God.

"You, God, are my God, earnestly I seek you; I thirst for you, my whole being longs for you, in a dry and parched land where there is no water" (Psalm 63:1).

He rewards those who earnestly seek him. (Hebrews 11:6b)

## Acknowledgement

Firstly, to My greatest friend and confidant Holy Spirit. You continue to reveal the Father and completed work of Jesus to me! Thank You for the insight and most importantly, YOUR LOVE!

Gary, my forever love, you are TRULY a God-sent. Thank you for being the best husband FOR ME!

Master Hebron, thank you son for teaching me a new level of faith, perseverance and going deeper into God's presence!

To my family and friends, your support and encouragement means everything.

## Table of Contents

| | |
|---|---:|
| Foreword | 11 |
| Introduction | 13 |
| One Thing Have I Desired | 19 |
| Wisdom Above All Else | 27 |
| I Was Blind But Now I See | 44 |
| Close Yet Far | 53 |
| You Have but ONE Job | 65 |
| Forgetting Those Things | 75 |
| Keeping the Main Thing | 86 |
| Prayer of Salvation | 96 |
| Biography | 98 |

# Foreword

As a relatively "new" entrepreneur, I can tell you from recent experience that when it comes to finding success, it's not about having all the right answers. Instead, it's about asking the right questions to God, myself and others.

Many of you may be embarking upon a new crossroad in your own life. Your focus may be all over the place right now. I submit to you that the main thing you need to focus on is Y.O.U. You need to know what you are made of, who you are, how you think and what your purpose is here on earth.

And that is why I am so glad that Charity wrote this book. "THIS ONE THING", is a gift from her heart to yours. This read will take you on a walk through the Word of God as well as a stroll through your life's journey to aid you in focusing on one thing at a time.

One of Charity's most outstanding characteristics is that of a prayer warrior! She is wise beyond her years of life as it relates to things of the spirit. She is a bonified communicator of truth and with this book, she will walk you through a step-by-step process in pursuit of His plan, priorities and promises for your life. So if you are desiring a thing, seeking wisdom, need to overcome in an area of lack, or in a season of repositioning yourself to walk boldly in your purpose....get ready to receive freedom as you open your heart, mind and spirit to this adventure.

As you navigate through your life, you will inevitably face obstacles, challenges and frustrating situations designed to get you off track. This book will equip you with a renewed sense of balance, peace and focus rooted in the Word of God. As we keep "This One Thing" as the main thing in our lives, we will be better able to walk out our destiny, fulfill our purpose and make this world a better place.

Kimberly T. Massey
Chief Empowerment Officer
Claim- Life Enterprises

# Introduction

I should be rich by now!

I should be married by now!

I should be out of debt by now!

I should be in shape by now!

I should be over this hurt by now!

Feel free to insert whatever your "by now" to this list! From to the least to the greatest, we all have had, at some point in our lives, those "by now" conversations with ourselves and others. As long as there is breath in our bodies, we have the supreme privilege to pursue our passions, live our best lives and create lasting memories.

While endeavoring to live our best lives, we can sometimes get caught up in competing to accomplish our goals and live the life we want! I believe we can agree that we live in a hyper competitive society. In the reality of a competing world, we all have been a part of this rat race. Whether knowingly or unknowingly, whether by choice or by force, whether directly or indirectly, each of us have be in some form of competition.

> *"Competition is the spice of sports; but if you make spice the whole meal, you'll be sick."*
> -George Leonard
>
> *"Competition brings out the best in products and the worst in people."*
> -David Sarnoff

We compete to be the best athlete. We compete to be the best worker. We compete to beat our best personal record. Seniors compete at nursing homes for the attention of the staff. At times, even our children compete for our attention! There is no age limit, no socioeconomic status, no race, no gender that precludes the big C. I've seen my toddler compete for his "perceived position" as the head honcho, AND HE'S ONLY TWO!

It does not matter if our intentions are pure or petty, the world of competition is here to stay! Though it is not always a negative thing, competition must be put in perspective and put in check.

While in hot pursuit of our goals and navigating the murky, shark-filled waters of competition, where does God fit into the equation? Is He at the epicenter of all we do or is He an emergency only fall back plan?

On our quest for more, we cannot become subtly snared in the "obtainment" that we lose focus on the Provider of said provision. Just in case it's not obvious, GOD is our ONLY source! All other things and people are resources that He ALLOWS to bless and enhance our lives. When we begin to look at our jobs, people and even ourselves as the source, we are dabbling into SOURCery (sorcery), as we are trying to meet our needs ***independent*** of God! Let that sink in for a minute!

This dark knowledge of meeting your own needs and being your provider is the norm for the world. This should NOT be for Kingdom citizens. The Word of God reminds us that we should not be conformed to this world but transformed (paraphrased).

> *Romans 12:2 (MSG) Don't become so well-adjusted to your culture that you fit into it without even thinking. Instead, fix your attention on God. You'll be changed from the inside out. Readily recognize what he wants from you, and quickly respond to it. Unlike the culture around you, always dragging you down to its level of immaturity, God brings the best out of you, develops well-formed maturity in you.*

WHEW!!! This is TOTAL opposite of the *"For the Culture"* phrase and movement that has been popularized in our generation. Trust me. This too shall pass and be replaced by something else! You know why? There's no lasting commitment in our society. It's a fad, a faze, a fleeting moment. This is just another reason why God tells us not to follow this world's way of doing things. It's faulty, flimsy and flippant fancies are here today and gone tomorrow. The instabilities are no way to build the foundations of the dreams, visions, purposes and destiny that God has given us. There is greatness inside each of us and in the words of my dear mother, it behooves us to get before God to get a better understanding of why we are here.

God will give us a glimpse of our destiny, give us a vision, a dream, a plan, a purpose and a goal to obtain. Knowing God the way I do and how He operates, He will give us an assignment, a vision, a dream, a destiny, a desire this is ASTRONOMICAL and much too big for us to do! There are three *natural* responses to what He has revealed:

(1)     Question – either we question if God even said it, was that the devil or was it our own thoughts; conversely, we question whether we can do it and how to do it.

(2)     Fight – we put on the boxing gloves and say come hell or high waters, we are going to make it happen by any means

necessary; we are not leaving this earth without seeing and hearing "mission accomplished."

(3)   Flight – we run from the assignment altogether; we say "ONE, TWO, THREE, NOT IT" and take off running like Usain Bolt!

I know it feels undaunting, but at this point, we have but ONE JOB….step into His presence for a download of instructions. In our excitement, we tend to move before time, or conversely when impaired by fear, we will not move at all.

Prioritizing God and abiding in His presence will be paramount to every move we make…before, during and after the assignment. Prioritizing God does not mean we pray first thing in the morning to show Him that He's #1 in our lives. N-O. He wants to be involved in EVERY aspect of our day and life! Prioritizing God means to consult Him on decisions BEFORE they are made, involving Him in every matter of the heart, seeking Him for guidance with family matters, asking Him about career moves, school choices and even taking promotions (remember the devil knows how to present counterfeits!).

As God provide the needful instructions to proceed, you will inevitably face challenges, oppositions, things and people who compete for your time, talent, attention and position. DO NO BITE THE BAIT, DO NOT WALK INTO THE LIGHT CAROLY

ANNE! You will hear God tell you more "ONE THING" instructions.

As you continue reading, you will find the references to the "ONE THING" moments that some of our favorite biblical heroes encountered.

1. One thing David desired
2. One thing Solomon requested
3. One thing the rich, young ruler lacked
4. One thing Martha needed
5. One thing the blind man knew
6. One thing Paul did

For me, these six scripture references point back to my need and deep dependence on prayer and constant fellowship with God. My very life depends on His direction. I take my guidance from His leading. Daily I seek Him, daily I serve Him, not because I have to, but because I get the pleasure to do so.

Let the journey begin!

# Chapter 1

# One Thing Have I Desired

*Psalm 27:4*

*One thing have I desired of the LORD, that will I seek after; that I may dwell in the house of the LORD all the days of my life, to behold the beauty of the LORD, and to enquire in his temple.*

## One Thing I Desire

If there is one place in the world that you could go to, all expenses paid, where would it be?

If you could work the occupation of your dreams, what would it be?

If you could have lunch with anyone, past or present, with whom would it be?

If you could have any amount of money, how would you spend it?

I can venture to say all of us have had desires and wishes, some of us more than others. Can any of us say that our desires consumed the very core of our existence? David could! Of all the things King David could have desired, and they were LEGITMATELY many, he wanted God's dwelling place more than anything and anyone. He wanted to be in the house of the Lord more than he wanted another wife or side piece (and you know how David LOVED the women folk! I'm just saying!), more than he wanted to be a forever ruler, more than his posterity, more than riches, more than fame, more than anything. In all of his pain, panic, confusion, distraction, and pressure, David narrows down his request to one thing! David somehow came to this place where even in light of everything he so desperately needed God to do . . . he was able to use laser-like focus and ask for one thing.

Think about it. This was during a time when David was hotly pursued by the enraged Saul and his bloodline (Saul's descendants and Abner), was a nomad, going from place to place for safety sake, was hated by his brothers, was scorned by his wife, was under siege by his own son Absalom, was treated with deep insolence (remember Nabal and even his own squad wanted to kill him at Ziglag). David could have asked for revenge and to be avenged. He could have asked for protection, peace and rest from his enemies; he could have even asked for an expanded kingdom for all the trouble he endured. All of those asks would have been justifiably understandable.

David did not even allow his title to make him usurp authority. He could have said "as the king, I desire to be with you in the holy of holies." However, he knew just to be in the building, in the area, in the presence of the great and awesome presence of the Great and Awesome God will give him everything he needed.

David no only desired to be in the house of the Lord but he sought after it. To seek signifies a striving after, to endeavor, to search diligently, to ask, desire, pray, make petition, request or to run down. David's seek and desire to be with God in His temple was not to merely go to the house of the Lord just to be going. His sole purpose was to love and be loved, to minister and be ministered to, to give and to receive, to pour out and to be poured back into even more!

One Thing I Desire

The scripture goes on to say "*...to behold the beauty of the Lord...*". The Hebrew translation of this reference to God's beauty is His glory, majesty, honor, excellency, goodly or transliterated *hadar*. Have you ever just stood in total awe of God? Ever been completely blown away by His majestic splendor? Left without words because of His grandeur and greatness yet compelled to try to express adoration through words of exultation, exhortation and exuberance. I imagine David feeling and thinking the same way. David *intimately knew* God as a deliverer (Goliath), protector (Saul), shepherd (trained by God Himself), and avenger (Nabal). These were not mere titles he heard his forefathers call God. As the saints of old would say, "this ain't what I heard, but what I know 'cuz I tried Him for myself." David can confidently testify that God is a counselor, sustainer, refuge, strong tower, buckler, shield, defense, lover of the soul, merciful, gracious, and all together wonderful. He's great, glorious, all-powerful, all-seeing, all-knowing, all-mighty, ever-present help, comforter, keeper, healer, a secret place, my hiding place, my shelter. Ok now I'm testifying! But that is what happens when we begin to reflect on the greatness of who our great God Jehovah El Elyon the Most High God is! Only an AWEsome God can take our breath away, leave us speechless and we still try to use a million words to BEGIN to describe the opulence of His magnanimous nature!

After David takes in the beauty (glory) of God, he said he will enquire in His temple. The Hebrew word for enquire is *baqar, which means "to find out all that constant fellowship or unbroken intercourse with God can teach."* Let that breathe and sink in for a minute! When you are in constant communion with God, there is an intimacy that transpires; transparency takes place. The deeper we go in our relationship with God, the more He begins to reveal things about ourselves and Him and about the inner workings of the Kingdom. Secrets are shared in this intimate space.

What we do not read in this passage is the hurriedness in this relationship. In a *healthy* relationship, it takes time to build up trust, truth and transparency before sharing some of the weightier matters of the heart, right? We do not just start telling our entire life stories and our life plans for the next 50 years in one sitting (AT LEAST IT IS PROBABLY NOT THE WISEST DECISION TO DO SO!). Well first natural, then spiritual. God is not going to share with you the secrets of creation because you all had one good conversation. NO! It is going to take much more than that but do know that He is more than ready AND willing to invest in this relationship.

Truth be told, God has been waiting for us to seek Him out to develop a more intimate relationship. Do you not know that He LONGS for deep intimacy with each of us? It is not reserved just for the elite people such as the pastors, prophets, and preachers. As much as God wants the time and personal relationship, He will not force us into it (He does use strongly suggested signs at times 😊).

## One Thing I Desire

He gives us the option to choose what we want to do. My prayer is that we make the right choice. Scripture tells us that in His presence is fullness of joy and at His right hand are pleasures forevermore. That sounds like a sum total of everything we could ever ask for, no matter how we construct the ask!

## **NOTES**

## One Thing I Desire

# Chapter 2

# Wisdom Above All Else

*1 Kings 3:9 (ESV)*

*Give your servant therefore an understanding mind to govern your people, that I may discern between good and evil,*

Can we all agree that we are in a time where we need godly leaders who will seek God for His wisdom and be surrounded by wise people who will give sound counsel and not be a fan, friend or flunky. From the president to the pastor, from Congress to the congregation, those in authority NEED wisdom from above, because it is apparent that man's "wisdom" has netted us next to nothing!

If leaders today were put in Solomon's position, what would have been their one request? If we were given this kind of blank check to God's unlimited resources, what would we fill it in with? Before you fix your mouth to lie, let me tell you MONEY is a pretty tempting option. A few million would settle a lot of my needs, wants and desires!

As leaders of nations, kings definitely needed wealth to maintain their kingdoms; they needed sufficient funding to cover military, the land and water pathways and palaces. The ruler could only raise so much from taxing the people before the country's economy took a nose dive, resulting in inflation, recession, depression and suppression (*HINT, HINT 21$^{ST}$ CENTURY!*). Power would be another good ask. It is easy to assume that a king, queen, or president would ask for money, power, triumphant victory over their enemies, peace in the land. Maybe even the request would be one for longevity and great a legacy or even great health. I'm sure some of us would use the one request for the furtherance of mankind, with having cures for cancer, the common cold and Crohn's disease to the total eradication of global starvation and the provision of clean water worldwide. Conversely, I am also undoubtedly sure that some would be tempted to use their one request for personal gain and ask for fame or beauty or strength or intelligence or would they ask for something that would be in the best interest of God and others?

One particular king in the Bible was given this opportunity that we all, at some point, have dreamed God would ask us at least once in life. His request, more than likely, was a little different than 99.9% of us. Solomon uttered none of those above wishes. Those requests/wishes are not bad, but they could not help Solomon fulfill the greatest part of his purpose, which was leading the people of Israel. Either money or power would have been great assets for Solomon as king, as most kings spent their reigns using one to get the other, and desperately doing whatever it takes to protect it.

Nevertheless, Solomon showed rare aptitude to see past this, which is evidenced in him asking God to give him wisdom, so that he may make the right decisions that will both honor God and help the people. He asked for wisdom because his desired was to please God and to serve God's people with the utmost honesty, integrity and justice. God strategically placed him as the head of this great nation of people so what he said and did affected many millions of people, and he showed his true heart by asking for help to do the right thing. It is also a humble response - Solomon is admitting that he is not able to do this on his own.

Following in the steps of his father King David, whose request was to dwell in God's presence, Solomon's request for wisdom and an understanding heart transcends personal profits and arrogant ambitions! Solomon's "one thing" moved beyond himself and focused on the people that God entrusted to him.

This request for wisdom was remarkable, given the circumstances in which he came into office. Solomon had just succeeded his father as the new king. In this rocky transition between monarchies, Solomon's older brother, Adonijah, made a run for the throne by trying to seize the sovereignty, while David was still alive! You are a cold piece of work to try and dethrone the king while fam was in hospice. Bruh, can you let him die FIRST before making a play for rulership? More importantly, it was NEVER yours to have! How about that sir! Please pardon me, I get caught up when discussing David's lineage!

David had to move expeditiously and make Solomon the new king, as he knew Adonijah was staging a coup! He quickly made Solomon King and had those loyal to him out together hosting a huge parade into Jerusalem to announce the real successor to throne. Adonijah's subjects disappeared when they found out that King David's supporters gave Solomon a royal public procession announcing his kingship, and Solomon succeeds in foiling the coup.

Although Adonijah vowed to stop the madness with trying to take the throne, he made one more attempt to undermine his father's directives and take the kingdom from Solomon. The end results of yet another failed attempt ended with heads rolling, figuratively and literally; those devoted to Adonijah were either executed or fired.

With all of that behind him, Solomon went on with the business of running the kingdom and one of the first orders of business was the massive thousand-animal sacrifice Solomon made to God. This act of worship touched the heart of God to the point where, later that night, God appeared to Solomon in a dream and said to him, "Ask for whatever you want Me to give you." That's when Solomon asked for wisdom.

Just like Solomon, we all need the wisdom of God to successfully navigate through this life. The teaspoon of wisdom that we have is limited and can only take us so far. With the moral fabric of our land deteorating before our eyes, we do not have the luxury to be chameleonlike, adapting and adjusting each time our surroundings change. We must inoculate ourselves with the wisdom of God and allow His truth, not our emotions and definitely not societal norms, be our compass.

The wisdom of God will help us apply the knowledge we have gained to make wise decisions. Brothers and sisters, do realize there is a *distinct* difference between wisdom, knowledge, understanding, discernment and insight. Each of these terms have been used interchangeably but each have their discrete variances in the essence of their meanings and their applications in our lives.

The presence of knowledge does not equate to the presence of wisdom. Knowledge is really about facts and ideas that we acquire through study, research, investigation, observation, or experience. I can do a Google search and have massive amounts of knowledge (information, data, facts), but I have not processed or reasoned what is actual and applicable to my life. Those with understanding are able to extract the meaning out of information. They "see through" the facts to the dynamics of what, how, and why. Understanding is a lens which brings the facts into crisp focus and produces principles. Discernment is deciphering and judging which aspects of that knowledge are true, just and righteous according to God's standard. Wisdom is the application of said knowledge, understanding and discernment. Insight is the profound plane of knowing and provides the greatest sense of understanding to our lives. Insight is a deeper and clearer perception of life, of knowledge, of wisdom. It is the essence of wisdom. Insight is a truer understanding of our lives and the bigger picture of how things all fit together.

Those with wisdom know which principle to apply in a given context. Understanding without wisdom can appear contradictory.

*Proverbs 26:4-5 – ⁴ Don't answer the foolish arguments of fools, or you will become as foolish as they are. ⁵ Be sure to answer the foolish arguments of fools, or they will become wise in their own estimation.*

Which principle to use depends on the context and situation. Those with wisdom know what actions to take next. They do the right thing in the given situation based on the leading of Holy Spirit.

Look at the terms this way:

*Knowledge* is my marathon practice long run is 22 miles.

*Understanding* is I need to pack enough water to last the run.

*Discernment* is I need to run my race, my pace, slow and steady while conserving my consumption of liquid.

*Wisdom* is I need to drink at least four ounces of water every 3 miles to stay hydrated and keep my pace.

*Insight* is having a stand that sells water, electrolyte drinks and potassium-booster snacks at mile 12.

One more for the road….

*Knowledge* is I received a $20,000 bonus from my job.

*Understanding* is how to manage the money with budgeting, spending, saving and investing.

*Discernment* is differentiating between a want and need or a good investment opportunity and a scam.

*Wisdom* is paying off the two lowest balanced credit cards, depositing a portion into savings, and investing in technology stock that you prayed about and researched.

*Insight* is realizing that money is simply a tool to be used, that it does not define who I am or my value (my net worth does not define or determine my self-worth!).

I am a "bottom line it" type of person in many situations so what helps me at times is summarizing information in as few words as possible. This table gives a very simplified 10,000 feet aerial view of the terms often associated, used interchangeably and sometimes mistaken for wisdom. The following table may help you visualize the difference between these three terms:

| Knowledge | Understand-ing | Discernment | Wisdom | Insight |
|---|---|---|---|---|
| Facts | Meaning | Accuracy of Facts | What to do next | How that affects my life |
| Information | Principles | Integrity of Information | Application | How to maximize the choices made |
| Memory | Reason | Judge the reasoning | Action | Create habit through repetition |

Do we need wisdom the same way Solomon did? I think the answer to this is a resounding yes! We may not make decisions which will affect millions, but we do choose a path which will affect those who are important to us - our children, our spouses, our extended families, our friends. If and since the wisdom of God is essential to survival and thriving in life, how do we obtain it? JUST ASK! I know it sounds like I have dramatically oversimplified it, but it starts with us asking God for wisdom. The Holy Spirit is ready to lavish it upon us. And do not be deceived by a popular concept that says experience is the best teacher. I VEHEMENTLY DISAGREE! Holy Spirit is THE BEST teacher. Does the experience from failed relationship after failed relationship teach us and prepare us for the next relationship or even marriage, as if the negative experience is needed to learn what not to do in the next? Does bankruptcy teach us to be better financial managers? Does failed business investments give the wisdom to successfully venture into the next business opportunity?

Experience *has the potential to* produce wisdom, however, for many people, experience does not give birth to wisdom, but deep cynicism and bitterness. Many learn mistrust, develop low expectations about the next relationship, and become trigger shy about investing themselves and resources again. In fact, repeated failures in love and life has a greater probability to predict future failure, because repetitive failure indicates an inability (or unwillingness) to reflect on and learn from experience.

The Holy Spirit is here to help us navigate every experience and weed through the emotions to come up with the best path to take going forward. The Word tells us that the Holy Spirit, who is the Spirit of truth, is here to lead and guide us.

> *John 14:26 – But the Helper, the Holy Spirit, whom the Father will send in My name, He will teach you all things, and bring to your remembrance all that I said to you.*
>
> *Luke 12:12 – for the Holy Spirit will teach you in that very hour what you ought to say."*
>
> *1 John 2:27 – As for you, the anointing which you received from Him abides in you, and you have no need for anyone to teach you; but as*

*His anointing teaches you about all things, and is true and is not a lie, and just as it has taught you, you abide in Him.*

God is waiting on us to open our mouth, mind and heart to ask, seek and pursue His wisdom. The scripture in 1 Kings notes, "It pleased the Lord that Solomon had asked this" (1 Kings 3:10). It is God's sheer pleasure to give wisdom to those who truly seek it.

> *Proverbs 2:6–8 (KJV)– [6] For the LORD giveth wisdom: out of His mouth cometh knowledge and understanding. [7] He layeth up sound wisdom for the righteous: He is a buckler to them that walk uprightly. [8] He keepeth the paths of judgment, and preserveth the way of His saints.*

God wants us to have knowledge of Him and what He expects of us. To obey Him, we have to have knowledge of His will, His way and His Word. But as equally important as having knowledge is having wisdom. Knowing facts about God and the Bible is not all there is to wisdom. Wisdom is a gift from God.

> *James 1:5 – If any of you lacks wisdom, you should ask God, who gives generously to all*

*without finding fault, and it will be given to you."*

God blesses us with wisdom in order for us to glorify Him and use the knowledge we have of Him.

When Solomon asked for wisdom, God responded to Solomon by not only answering his request for wisdom but also favoring him with things that he did not even request.

1. Wisdom: "I now do according to Your word. Behold, I give you a wise and discerning mind, so that none like you has been before you and none like you shall arise after you" (verse 12). First Kings 4:29-34 records the details of Solomon's wisdom: "And God gave Solomon wisdom and understanding beyond measure, and breadth of mind like the sand on the seashore, so that Solomon's wisdom surpassed the wisdom of all the people of the east and all the wisdom of Egypt. For he was wiser than all other men, wiser than Ethan the Ezrahite, and Heman, Calcol, and Darda, the sons of Mahol, and his fame was in all the surrounding nations. He also spoke 3,000 proverbs, and his songs were 1,005. He spoke of trees, from the cedar that is in Lebanon to the hyssop that grows out of the wall. He spoke also of beasts, and of birds, and reptiles, and of fish. And people of all nations came to hear the wisdom of

Solomon, and from all the kings of the earth, who had heard of his wisdom."

2. Wealth: "I give you also what you have not asked, both riches and honor, so that no other king shall compare with you, all your days" (1 Kings 3:13). Solomon would become known as the wealthiest king of his era.

3. Longevity: a long life based on Solomon's obedience: "And if you will walk in my ways, keeping my statutes and my commandments, as your father David walked, then I will lengthen your days" (1 Kings 3:14).

When we make a quality decision to live life in accordance to God's will and way *daily*, we will grow in wisdom.

> *James 3:13-18 – ¹³ Who is wise and understanding among you? Let him show it by his good life, by deeds done in the humility that comes from wisdom. ¹⁷ But the wisdom that comes from heaven is first of all pure; then peace-loving, considerate, submissive, full of mercy and good fruit, impartial and sincere.*

Although wisdom is available to all who ask, not everyone wants wisdom or do what is necessary to obtain it, because they want to follow their emotions, and they also want the excuse of ignorance when their foolish behavior catches up to them. We must recognize that wisdom often runs contrary to EMOTION! At times, walking in wisdom will having you looking foolish. It does not appear wise to keep your mouth shut while someone is speaking foolishly about and to you (Proverbs 26:4; Matthew 5:44). It makes no sense to "turn the other cheek" when someone hits you (Matthew 5:38-40). It seems outright crazy to love those who hate us, speak blessings on those who curse us (Luke 6:27-36). It seems contradictory to praise God while in jail (Acts 16:25).

> *1 Corinthians 1:27 – But God hath chosen the foolish things of the world to confound the wise; and God hath chosen the weak things of the world to confound the things which are mighty;*

> *1 Corinthians 2:14 – But the natural man receiveth not the things of the Spirit of God: for they are foolishness unto him: neither can he know them, because they are spiritually discerned.*

When we seek God for His wisdom, not only will he point us to His Word, He will also connect us with wise people. There is much that we can learn by associating with wise people. As the old adage goes, you become like those who you hang around.

> *Proverbs 13:20 – "He who walks with the wise grows wise, but a companion of fools suffers harm."*

# NOTES

## Charity Morris

# Chapter 3

# One Thing I Know...
# I Was Blind But Now I See

*John 9:25*

*"but I know this: I was blind, and now I see!"*

If you had to forfeit the use of one of your senses for a week, which one would it be: Seeing, hearing, tasting, touching or smelling? Would you spend that time complaining about your temporary disability? Would you let everyone know what a sacrifice your life was under as a result of this inconvenience? Would you be even more grateful for that sense when it returned?

*Imagine being unable to enjoy the majestic scenery of a sunrise or sunset.*

*Imagine not being able to visually experience the beautiful array of flowers as they bloom in Spring or the vibrant colors of the trees as they change in the Fall.*

*Imagine being unable to experience unexplainable love and joy through the smile of a child.*

*Imagine not having sight or visions of pictures/images while dreaming (sleep mode).*

*Imagine being blind yet having to use your imagination to pen the words to "Isn't She Lovely?"*

To embody the character he was portraying, a blind singer and musician, an actor allowed himself to become blind for a period of time. These prosthetics were worn 24/7, before, during and after filming. In an interview, the actor stated, "Visualize having your

## I Was Blind

eyes glued shut for 14 hours a day; that's your jail sentence." To make matters worse, his colleagues kept forgetting that he couldn't see, and would, for example, leave him sitting alone at a table after lunch on the assumption that he could get back to the set on his own. Initially, he suffered from panic attacks until he became accustomed to the lightless lifestyle.

Whether low vision or no vision, being blind has to be a colossal challenge. It is definitely not a death sentence, it is, however, a "learn how to do things differently" life that has to be lived. This lifestyle is one that takes patience, persistence and endurance with learning and adjusting. The trust factor, as I imagine, has to be at an all-time high, as there is deep dependence on technology, people and even animals to help the blind person live life.

I remember when my husband got glasses for the first time. It was not until they ran the battery of tests and gave him a prescription to help the areas of his vision that were weak and lacking. When he put on those glasses, it was an entirely new world for him! Things became so much clearer and brighter. His vision was focused! One of his first comments was "how was I able to see without these?"

To see properly, our eyes and our brains must work together. The brain processes the images the eyes send it and recognize what it is being shown. In eyes that are functioning properly, this process is nearly instantaneous. Remember the eye-brain connection as we continue down this path. As it goes it the natural, so too the spirit. If what we constantly see is the issues, problems, challenges, circumstances, negativity or nothing at all, I will venture to say we are operating in a level of darkness/blindness/low vision; there's a spiritual misfiring taking place, as the wrong images are being projected and seen, and transmitted to the mind. The Word says that satan has blinded the eyes of the mind to truth.

> *2 Corinthians 4:4 ⁻ In their case the god of this world has blinded the minds of the unbelievers, to keep them from seeing the light of the gospel of the glory of Christ, who is the image of God.*

This word "minds" is the Greek word *noema* is not talking about the physical mind, but the thoughts, reasoning, opinions, feelings, beliefs, and views that a person holds. With that in mind, we can look at the context of the scripture as stating that satan has "gouged out" the spiritual eyes of skeptics and unbelievers to such a degree that *it has affected their ability to see things correctly*. Their *thoughts, reasoning, opinions, feelings, beliefs,* and *views* of what they experience and perceive are obstructed, hindered, and impeded. As a result, they are *blinded* from a correct *view* of the way things really are.

## I Was Blind

Oh but thank God for Jesus! For this purpose was the Son of God manifest to destroy the works of the evil one (1 John 3:8)! ALL of us at some point in life were blind and in gross darkness. We were blind to our destiny, destination, and most importantly the truth of God and His Word. Whether the blindness is a result of choices we have ignorantly made or as a result of improper teaching and modeling, Jesus is here to bring light and proper vision. We can look at how Jesus healed the blind man in John 9. Jesus literally and figuratively changed the way this man saw the world, both naturally and spiritually, and Jesus has done the same thing for many of us and is willing to do that for ALL.

Jesus and his disciples were walking saw a blind man begging on the side of the street. The disciples, the inquisitive miscreants that they were, asked Jesus a common question that most of us ask when we have challenges in life – "Who sinned?" Back then and even today, it was a very common belief to adopt that if someone was born with a disability or is facing storm after storm in life, it was a punishment from God as a result of sin.

Jesus answered that it was no one's fault and the next words Jesus had spoken are key… "This happened so that the work of God might be displayed in his life." At times, God will *allow* certain things to transpire in our life for a greater purpose of showcasing His power and glory. No it does not feel good, no it does look good but in the end, it will be good! Trust the plan and the process! God was going to do something special in this man's life, something big, something out of the ordinary – and being born blind was part of God's process for him.

Then Jesus forms mud by spitting in some dirt on the ground, put the mud on the blind man's eyes, and told him to go and wash in Siloam, which means *sent*. Now indulge me for a moment...I can handle many things, *BUT SPIT*...your girl cannot stomach it! Can you imagine someone spitting in the dirt, forming a mud clump and then coming towards you with that? Yes he was blind but he could hear! As a child, the quickest way to get me to give you something was to either spit on it or lick it! For me, this was one of the most unorthodox methods Jesus used to perform a miracle. He's spoken to storms, laid hands, and even spoken the word only and the miracle manifested. THIS TIME, He decided to use *spit!* As much as that grosses me out, think about the magnitude and power in that. The very One who created man, took His DNA and mixed it dirt, which is what was used to create man, and restored that man back to His original blueprint for vision!

The blind man obeyed and for the first time in his life, he was able to see! The power behind this miracle is not only is the man able to see but look how God restored or even replaced the eye-brain connection that helps to produce images. God supernaturally advanced his vision to that of a properly functioning adult. God could have given him the sight of an infant and had him

## I Was Blind

to grow and develop to full vision over time or He could have allowed him to adjust to processing of receiving light and images for the first time with brain misfires and needful "rewiring", as is the case with some people who have surgical procedures to restore sight.

In addition to restoring his physical vision, Jesus took care of fixing his spiritual blindness as well; the eyes of this man's spirit were still blind to THE TRUTH. When those hypocritical Pharisees, who walked in blindness themselves, challenged the validity of this man's miracle, he had no idea who had healed him. You know who those Pharisees are…these are our church-going folks who refuse to accept God's handiwork in our lives. We are no longer the same; Christ came and radically changed our lives, but they are trying to keep us bound to our past!

This man shut them down in one sentence, "One thing I know, I was blind but now I see." They were so prideful and indignant that they put him out of the church! Now Jesus reappears on this scene to give the greatest sight to have! Jesus asked the former blind man if he believed in the Son of Man. "Tell me who he is," the man said. Jesus said, "You're looking at him. Then the man said, 'Lord, I believe,' and he worshiped him." The man became a believer in the Lord Jesus Christ. EYES OPENED! With his brand-new eyes of faith, he saw Jesus for who He really was – the Son of God, the Savior of the mankind, Redeemer of the world.

# **NOTES**

## I Was Blind

# Chapter 4

# Close Yet Far

*Mark 10:21 (TLB)*

*Jesus felt genuine love for this man as he looked at him. "You lack only one thing," he told him; "go and sell all you have and give the money to the poor—and you shall have treasure in heaven—and come, follow me.*

Over the years, I have learned to embrace constructive feedback from people, whether solicited or unsolicited (never mind what my husband says!). If after coming to Jesus and asking Him for an assessment of what I am doing He tells me you only lack one thing, I honestly would be head over heels happy! My heart's desire is to live a life that is pleasing and acceptable unto Him. I aim to represent God well on this Earth so if He tells me, there's only one more thing for you to do, BABY, IT'S ON! However, if I were to be brutally honest with myself and seriously examine my life, I realize that there are MANY things that I am lacking, not just one. In fact, what I should probably do is make a list of things that keep me from God and from being the Christian that He wants me to be, and start working with one and then proceed to the rest. **DISCIPLINE!!!**

None of us likes to hear about our imperfections, inadequacies, areas of improvement, or opportunities for growth. Pick the phrase that makes you most comfortable! The point is, we all have to embrace growth and development if we want to attain better in life. Some of us rarely and *genuinely* enquire "What can I do to improve," because what is on the other side of that question exposes "weaknesses", "frailties," and "vulnerabilities;" the response will let us know that not only we have deficiencies but that they are recognized by others. It is pride and a self-protective stance that keeps us from asking the question, and pride that will keep us from heeding the potential answer.

In Mark 10, the rich, young ruler came to Jesus for an evaluation, if you will. He wanted to know what he can do improve an already great life by gaining eternal life.

> *Mark 10:17-23 (MSG) – [17] As he went out into the street, a man came running up, greeted him with great reverence, and asked, "Good Teacher, what must I do to get eternal life?" [18-19] Jesus said, "Why are you calling me good? No one is good, only God. You know the commandments: Don't murder, don't commit adultery, don't steal, don't lie, don't cheat, honor your father and mother." [20] He said, "Teacher, I have—from my youth—kept them all!" [21] Jesus looked him hard in the eye—and loved him! He said, "There's one thing left: Go sell whatever you own and give it to the poor. All your wealth will then be heavenly wealth. And come follow me." [22] The man's face clouded over. This was the last thing he expected to hear, and he walked off with a heavy heart. He was holding on tight to a lot of things, and not about to let go.*

Reading that last verse in the Message translation really makes it plain...*the rich, young ruler was holding on tight to his money and not about to let go!* It was *his* possessions, *his* wealth, *his* money and he had ZERO interest in parting ways with it. Even though he had fulfilled many, if not most of the commandments, he violated the first commandment, "Thou shall have no other gods before me" (Exodus 20:3). Verse 23 tells us that he became very sad for he had great possessions (KJV).

The task of selling everything would not, in itself, give eternal life. In this particular case, Jesus asked the rich, young ruler to give away his wealth because he was more concerned with his possessions than he was with following Jesus. Wealth, not God, consumed his life. What this person lacked was an undivided loyalty to God.

Having money is not intrinsically bad so do not get nervous, Jesus is not asking us to sell all that we have! TAKE A DEEP BREATH! He will, however, require each of us to rid ourselves of anything that has become or that can potentially become more important than God. He wants us to remain focused by removing from our life anything that could shift our attention away from Him.

Now grant it, my financial status is not quite the same as the rich, young ruler RIGHT NOW, but I choose to believe money is not my choking point (Lord, just do not put me in an Abraham and Isaac situation with my Hebron). If I were in that situation, how would I have responded? If I were in my 20s and was a multimillionaire, multi-platinum recording artist who received my first Grammy, American Music Award, and Billboard Music Award by 19, my first Tony by 22, my first Emmy by 25 and an Oscar by 29, how would I react had I received the message to sell all that I have? What if I were a triple threat athlete: tennis, track, and golf and became so great at each that I went pro in all three, earning me millions in tournaments and endorsements; what would be my response to the phrase sell what you have and follow me? What if I were a quickly rising force in the political arena, having had the office of a Congresswoman by the age of 23, state senator by 30 and now headed to be a gubernatorial candidate by the age of 40? Would I readily give up the power and position of politics to follow Jesus?

Yours and my one thing may not be money. For some of us it is power, for others it is ambition, sexual behavior, or hatred. What is that one thing we still lack in our life? Is it some sin we refuse to let go? Is it some part of our life we refuse to surrender to God? Is it some love we place above our love for Christ? Is it some person we refuse to forgive? The challenge is that we do not trust God and we want to hold back something extra for ourselves because we believe that we cannot live (or live as comfortably) without it. That one thing we still lack is like a certain room in our house that we do not want God to enter. We keep the door shut and locked, making it a sacred, untouchable place. "God, you can have everything, but not this one thing! You can enter any room of my house, but not this one!" By doing this we make an idol of that one department of our life.

Money, fame, and power may not be our choking points, but I can guarantee you, there is something lurking that will certainly at least give you a cause to pause if Jesus asked you that question. Jesus' message has not changed from the time He told the rich, young ruler to today and that is detach from your earthly possessions and attach to Me. Let go of what's in your hand and take My hand. His greatest need was not the selling of his possession but the need for eternal life from Jesus, something that no amount of fame, fortune, or favor we possess can buy.

Why do you think Jesus told this young man to give up what he had and follow Him? I believe Jesus wanted to show this man a new way of operating and living. Not only was he going to gain eternal life, Jesus was going to show him how to work on a new level, according to Kingdom principles. Let me prove it to you. Peter, James and others were fishermen. Did not Jesus supernaturally bring in the greatest catch of fish they had ever seen, with NO TOIL?

> *Luke 5:4-10 (NLT) – [4] When he had finished speaking, he said to Simon, "Now go out where it is deeper, and let down your nets to catch some fish."*

*⁵ "Master," Simon replied, "we worked hard all last night and didn't catch a thing. But if you say so, I'll let the nets down again." ⁶ And this time their nets were so full of fish they began to tear! ⁷ A shout for help brought their partners in the other boat, and soon both boats were filled with fish and on the verge of sinking.*

*⁸ When Simon Peter realized what had happened, he fell to his knees before Jesus and said, "Oh, Lord, please leave me—I'm such a sinful man." ⁹ For he was awestruck by the number of fish they had caught, as were the others with him. ¹⁰ His partners, James and John, the sons of Zebedee, were also amazed.*

Matthew was a tax collector. Did not Jesus have Peter go and pull money out of a fish to pay taxes?

*Matthew 17:27 – go down to the shore and throw in a line, and open the mouth of the first fish you catch. You will find a coin to cover the taxes for both of us; take it and pay them.*

Whether the rich, young ruler gained his wealth through inheritance or ingenuity, he had a divine appointment with the Master to experience a new dimension, a transcendence from self-righteousness and works to the gift of grace! Sadly, he did not see the treasure in Christ as much as he saw in his earthly treasures.

Tragically the rich, young ruler's great possessions proved to possess him! They were an obstacle to having the Pearl of Greatest Price, the wealth and wisdom that can only come from following Christ.

We can have everything this age has to offer, but without Jesus, we still lack the one thing that matters most. If we gain the whole universe, and have not Jesus, we are infinitely impoverished compared to the One who has The TRUE Treasure. There is no amount of coinage, celebrity status, or accomplishments that will cause us to acquire God's acceptance; none of this will satisfy the longing and hole in the soul. Receiving awards will not suffice. Having chart-topping hits will not be enough. Winning championships will not be as satisfying. Personal success will not do. Massive amounts of wealth, fame, friends, and a large social-media following will not bring contentment. Even the church/body of Christ is suffering from a Hollywood, fame, accolades hyper social need-for-applause environment. One of my many challenges with the church today is that we want to witness to and win the world yet too much of the world can be identified in the church! The Body is lacking a complete and total commitment to Christ in every aspect. We want to hold onto to Jesus and hold onto the things of this world at the same time. That is not going to work! Reckless abandonment is required, like that of Apostle Paul when he stated it's all dung in comparison to knowing Jesus.

Philippians 3:7-12 (MSG) – [7-9] The very credentials these people are waving around as something special, I'm tearing up and throwing out with the trash—along with everything else I used to take credit for. And why? Because of Christ. Yes, all the things I once thought were so important are gone from my life. Compared to the high privilege of knowing Christ Jesus as my Master, firsthand, everything I once thought I had going for me is insignificant—dog dung. I've dumped it all in the trash so that I could embrace Christ and be embraced by him. I didn't want some petty, inferior brand of righteousness that comes from keeping a list of rules when I could get the robust kind that comes from trusting Christ—*God's* righteousness.

[10-11] I gave up all that inferior stuff so I could know Christ personally, experience his resurrection power, be a partner in his suffering, and go all the way with him to death itself. If there was any way to get in on the resurrection from the dead, I wanted to do it.

¹² I'm not saying that I have this all together, that I have it made. But I am well on my way, reaching out for Christ, who has so wondrously reached out for me.

One of the beautiful truths we can learn from the rich, young ruler and the Apostle Paul is that we are saved by grace, but grace necessitates a retort from the receiver. Accepting this gift of grace needs a commitment, a total surrender from each of us. God paid the ultimate price by giving His Son and the Son paid the ultimate price by giving His life, but They expect us, in return, to give ourselves. Grace is free but is in no way inexpensive. It came at a great price. We can never pay for it, earn it or deserve it.

The deeper message, though, is that all of us have something more in our lives — one more thing with which God wants to deal. No matter how far we have come, no matter how much we have matured, no matter how much we think we know, there is still "one thing" we lack. What has Jesus put His finger on in our life? Has the Spirit of God reminded us of some issue, some lack? Let God rummage around deep inside our heart. Everyone else may think we have it all together. We may look okay on the outside, but allow God to come along, peel back the layers, and say, "What about this?" Will we respond like this wealthy man, walking away, shutting out God's deeper work or will we surrender to Jesus' ongoing work of grace within our heart?

# NOTES

## Close Yet Far

# Chapter 5

# You Have but ONE Job

*Luke 10:41–42*

*But the Lord answered her, "Martha, Martha, you are anxious and troubled about many things, but one thing is necessary. Mary has chosen the good portion, which will not be taken away from her."*

## You Have ONE Job

My beautiful sister in love Alexis has a schedule that will make the average person faint...between home schooling, parenting three amazing children, wife to a husband with a demanding schedule and an entrepreneur in her own rights, no one can argue that she is busy. In a world that is drawing her in to be a Martha, she has sweetly managed to develop the Mary in her by purposely sitting at the feet of the Master and gleaning from His life-refreshing, love-imparting words.

Many of us can identify with the busy lifestyle of my sister Alexis. In a culture of hectic schedules and the relentless pursuit of productivity, we are tempted to measure our worth by how busy we are, by how much we accomplish, or by how well we meet the expectations of others. In progressive organizations, more flexible work models are being introduced to the workers, where they are able to do their work remotely. This is a difficult concept for some managers, as they need to "see" their team busy working to prove their worth. I can look busy and not be productive but that is the wickered mindset that many have bought into...if we appear busy, you must be working.

Just as organizations are making accommodations for busy lifestyles, so too are we looking for ways to manage our overly busy lives. The hustle and bustle of this world will take us out if we do not properly plan and prepare for it. Some married couples even have to schedule time to make love (no judgement here)!

The busyness of life is nothing new. In Luke 10, Martha, the sister of Lazarus and Mary had an unexpected houseguest—the Son of God. Martha was distracted by all the preparations, which she felt had to be made. Just imagine, God Himself is visiting. The house is a mess. The food is not ready. The table is dirty. God is sitting in your living room, and your sister refuses to help!

Now you know 99% of the times, Jesus had a crowd of people following him, so it was very probably that others were with him, in addition to His goon squad, the disciples. It is similar to the house parties we used to have back in the day! You invited a group of people but by the time it is over, there are a number of people you do not know *and* did not invite who came to the party! This could have very well been Martha's plight!

Keep in mind, hospitality was extremely important during this era. When Jesus came to Bethany, Martha showed hospitality by welcoming Jesus into her home. She then busies herself with the tasks of serving their guest (*diakonian*). Although we are not told precisely what those tasks are, a good guess is that she began preparing a meal. While she toils over a meal for Jesus and others, Mary sits at Jesus' feet, listening to His words. Rather than assuming the role expected of women in their culture, she takes her place at the feet of Jesus. She assumes the posture of a student learning at the feet of a rabbi, a role customarily earmarked for men.

There are three things to note about Mary: (1) Posture, (2) Position, and (3) Priority. Posture – Mary was sitting on the ground. We are not talking about tiled, hardwood or carpeted flooring. She is on the ground with dirt and bugs but that did not seem to be a problem for her! Was it comfortable, probably not, but that did not matter. Receiving from the matter was all that mattered. Position – Mary was at the feet of Jesus. This signifies humility and gives reverential homage to her mentor and Master. Priority – Mary could have given herself to be hospitable like her sister Martha, but she made a different choice *(this choice is at the core of all we must do…choose this day whom ye will serve!)*. She discerned the weightier need in her life and tended to that by sitting at the feet of Jesus and receiving every Word He had said. Mary chose to serve Jesus by allowing Him to serve her the Words of life!

> *Proverbs 4:20–21 – My son, give attention to my words; incline your ear to my sayings. Do not let them depart from your eyes; keep them in the midst of your heart;*

What I absolutely LOVE about this passage of scripture is the evidenced RELATIONSHIP each of them had with Jesus. Mary's *actions* demonstrated an established relationship and Martha's *spoken words* demonstrated an established relationship. Martha, who was distracted by her many tasks, approached Jesus and asked, "Lord, do you not care that my sister has left me to do all the work by myself? Tell her then to help me" (Luke 10:40). You do no say that to a house guest you are entertaining for the first time! That's numero uno. Secondly, the tone in which she said it denotes a level of comfort to come at <u>MY</u> Savior like that! You MUST know Him!

The issue with Martha is not that she is busy serving and have given herself to hospitality. Undoubtedly, Jesus praises this kind of service, notably in the parable of the Good Samaritan that immediately precedes the story of Mary and Martha. The problem with Martha is not her serving, but rather that she is **worried and distracted**. The Greek translation for the word "distracted" in verse 40, *periespato,* means to be pulled or dragged in multiple directions.

Martha's distraction and worry forsook the primary tenants of hospitality, which is gracious attention to the guests. She forgets all of the Emily Post etiquette rules by attempting to sister shame Mary in front of everyone, including the guest of honor. Martha must have really been at her wits end to *accuse* her house guest of not caring about what she's trying to do for them and then *ask*s him to intercede in a family dispute. That's gutsy and insane at the same time! Get yo' life Martha!

Martha's worry and distraction disallowed her from being in the moment with her friend, The Savior Jesus. She has missed out on the "one thing needed" for true hospitality. There is no greater hospitality than spending time with and listening to your guest. How much more so when the guest is Jesus! Jesus responded to her complaint by saying, "You are anxious and troubled with much serving." Martha was so focused on doing a good thing that she missed out on the best thing.

Had Martha joined Mary, everything else could have been covered. The miracle of multiplication had already happened so Jesus could have easily multiplied what they already had available to feed everyone there. MISSED OPPORTUNITIES!

Many people can see the Martha in themselves. With distinct feeling of being dragged in different directions, there is a resounding recurring theme of worry and distraction that touches all of our lives. The constant warring with worrying and open invitation to distractions of all sorts lures us to busy ourselves with the cares of this world and yet, as Jesus says in Luke 12:25 *(Amp)*, *"And which of you by being overly anxious and troubled with cares can add a cubit to his stature or a moment [unit] of time to his age [the length of his life]?"* We ALL know (at least we will after today) that worrying has **_ZERO_** redeeming qualities. It ages us, causes physical and mental distress, produces anxiety, causes sexual dysfunction, lends itself to over or undereating, produces panic attacks, causes sleeplessness, produces forgetfulness, and so much more. Truth be told, that which people are worried about is small in the grand scheme of things. It pales in comparison to the overall plan that God has and it is a mini freak-out because that person is no longer in control of the situation. There, I said it!

For the majority of us, our busyness and distraction stems from the best of intentions. There are plans, goals, and destinies we want to accomplish for the greater good of others; it's not just about selfish ambition. Our desire is to care for our families with needful provision and not in excess. My husband and I desire to give our children opportunities that produce growth and development spiritually, physically, mentally, socially, culturally, and economically. We want them to do things that we did not and could not do at that age.

Additionally, many of us desire to make a positive impact in our local church and community through service. The local body would not be able to function without volunteers, without those helping hands....THE MARTHA'S! These are your faithful team of people who serve in various ministries, from the Greeter to Missions Ministry. They give of themselves without asking for a return. These "faithful few" are extremely pivotal to making the church a welcoming and well-functioning community. The challenge is that these faithful few are used so much it can lead to busyness and burnout!

If left unchecked, all of these good works can leave us with no time to be still in the Lord's presence and hear God's Word. We are likely to end up worried and troubled and with a kind of service that is lacking in love and delight and is resentful of and to others. Let us not allow what we do for God replace the time we spend with God.

We do know that Jesus invites all of us who are worried and distracted by many things to sit at His feet and rest in His presence. This open invitation is for each of us to hear His affirming words of grace and truth, to know that we are loved and valued as children of the Most High God. Jesus is calling us into His presence to be renewed in faith and strengthened for service. There is need of only one thing: attention to our Guest. As it turns out, our Guest is also our Host, the Master and Savior of the World and He comes bearing gifts!

# NOTES

# You Have ONE Job

# Chapter 6

# Forgetting Those Things

*Philippians 3:13*

*Beloved, I do not consider that I have made it my own; but this **one thing** I do: forgetting what lies behind and straining forward to what lies ahead,*

Forgetting Those Things

People who know me well knows that, outside of Jesus, Apostle Paul is my biblical hero and mentor! His writings are epically inspiring and helps me in EVERY situation I face. Paul's life is a poster child of "If God can use him, he can use me." The zealot that was once a terrorist to the Christians, the original Isis, Bin Laden, and Kim Jong-Un all wrapped into one flesh was converted and set ablaze for the Master's use and oh how God used him!

Once Jesus radically saved him, there was no turning back! With the same passion, same zeal, same fervor, Paul advanced the Kingdom of God through teaching and preaching and performing many miracles. The signs, wonders and miracles that manifested through Paul came at a great price! He was no stranger to persecution. The ridicule not only came from the outside but also from the inside, fellow believers. Jealousy if you ask me!

Paul's desire to serve and please the Lord was so great that he did not mind suffering.

> *Philippians 4:10 – That I may know Him, and the power of his resurrection, and the fellowship of His sufferings, being made conformable unto His death;*

> *2 Corinthians 4:8-12 (MSG) – we've been spiritually terrorized, but God hasn't left our*

*side; we've been thrown down, but we haven't broken. What they did to Jesus, they do to us—trial and torture, mockery and murder; what Jesus did among them, He does in us—He lives! Our lives are at constant risk for Jesus' sake, which makes Jesus' life all the more evident in us. While we're going through the worst, you're getting in on the best!*

He did not mind the things he had to go through, because he knew it was for the sake of the call that was on his life. Paul was relentless in his passionate pursuit of God's presence. So great was his conviction that he said, *"and nothing will be able to separate him from the love of God."*

> *Romans 8:35-39 (TLB) – $^{35}$ Who then can ever keep Christ's love from us? When we have trouble or calamity, when we are hunted down or destroyed, is it because he doesn't love us anymore? And if we are hungry or penniless or in danger or threatened with death, has God deserted us? $^{36}$ No, for the Scriptures tell us that for his sake we must be ready to face death at every moment of the day—we are like sheep awaiting slaughter; $^{37}$ but despite all this,*

> *overwhelming victory is ours through Christ who loved us enough to die for us. [38] For I am convinced that nothing can ever separate us from his love. Death can't, and life can't. The angels won't, and all the powers of hell itself cannot keep God's love away. Our fears for today, our worries about tomorrow, [39] or where we are—high above the sky, or in the deepest ocean—nothing will ever be able to separate us from the love of God demonstrated by our Lord Jesus Christ when he died for us.*

Paul's longing to see the will of God manifested on the earth consumed every fiber of his being. His eye and heart stayed singularly focused on the Father. The apostle Paul was one who could talk from experience about singleness of his purpose. His 'one thing' appears in Philippians 3.

> *Philippians 3:13-14 – [13]Beloved, I do not consider that I have made it my own; but this **one thing** I do: forgetting what lies behind and straining forward to what lies ahead, [14] I press toward the goal for the prize of the upward call of God in Christ Jesus.*

What a powerful statement! For most of us, this is easier said than done! Forgiveness is one hurdle to overcome, forgetting the past altogether is a totally different chasm to conquer but look at the resolve and focus of Paul. He summed up his life in Christ as involving the perpetual forgetting of 'what was behind,' or simply put, his past, while uncompromisingly centering his energies and interests on the course that was ahead of him.

One thing that Paul did not do was shy away from his past. Not that he pretended like the past never happened but that he wasn't going to allow it to affect his present or dictate his future. Paul's past was quite colorful:

- He persecuted Christians
- He was beaten.
- He was flogged.
- He was stoned and left for dead
- He was talked about and accused, even by Christians.
- He was persecuted.
- He felt the cold sting of jealousy by the church folks.
- He was made to feel as if he didn't belong in the church because he didn't do things the way everybody else did.
- He was shipwrecked multiple times.
- He was bitten by a poisonous snake.

## Forgetting Those Things

The past also includes past successes and the good that has happened. Paul said:

- "I have had a lot of things. I am a Hebrew of the Hebrews. I had a wonderful education. I sat at the feet of Gamaliel, the greatest teacher of my generation. I did everything right as far as the law is concerned. I have kept the law from my youth, like the rich young ruler."
- He received visitations from the Lord Jesus Christ Himself,
- He chartered several churches throughout the Greek, Roman and Asian nations
- He wrote many epistles from the revelations the Lord had given to him
- He experienced the salvation and the infilling of the Holy Spirit with thousands of converts
- He witnessed to some of the top political people of that time
- Many signs, wonders and miracles were done through his ministry.

Paul said he must move past his past. No matter how good or bad things were, he did not allow himself to remain there. He did not allow all the wrong that happened to him to prevent him from moving forward in his assignment to reach people. Neither did he build an altar and remain at the place where he had experienced those great moves of God.

Paul said not only will I forget but I will press forward. When I hear press, I immediately this of exerting a force and expending energy to move. I will push past the pain and press toward the mark. It may not be easy, but my purpose is at stake. I may have to cry sometimes, but my goal is greater. I may be forsaken by those that say they will be by my side, but my desire to please God far outweighs this temporary inconvenience.

The literal translations for press is to seek after eagerly, earnestly endeavor, to acquire. One way the Holy Spirit expands certain meanings for me is through acronyms. He gave me one for press.

**P**ush through
**R**esistance
**E**xcuses
**S**etbacks and
**S**tumbling blocks

It does not matter what has happened in the past, PRESS through it. Press through those things that try to resist our advancement. Press past those life moments that lure us to use them as excuses to be stay stuck in the past. Yes, that firing was unjust. Yes, that divorce was painful. Yes, that breakup was devastating. Yes, the loss of a child was gut-wrenching. Absolutely, that rape was shameful. Yes, your neighbor was undeniably wrong for molesting your child. Yes sis, the loss of your edges was mortifying, yet we will not allow the devil to use these situations as setbacks to keep us stagnant and in prison to our past. If the enemy cannot keep you hostage to the past, he will definitely try to use annoyances to cause you to stumble. We have all had to deal with criticism from others, been the subject of hot gossip, been falsely accused. Press past these stumbling blocks! There's a higher goal to reach. We must fulfill our purpose; therefore, we are forgetting those things that are behind and we are going to P.R.E.S.S. toward the mark. We **_WILL_** push through resistance, excuses, setbacks and stumbling blocks!

Those thoughts of revenge forget it and move forward.

That feeling of rejection from the church folk that makes you feel like not even coming to church, we have got to forget it and press forward.

That anger that you have because the people have made you upset you must forget it and keep going.

Forgetting past hurts, offenses, problems, and failures is necessary in order to genuinely press toward the mark of Christ-likeness. We should learn from life's injuries, not be held captive by them. Forgetting is often the prerequisite to going forward. As we follow the example of the Apostle Paul and echo his words of "this one thing I do," let's not miss the truth that in order to reach ahead and press forward it is necessary to forget some things. Remember, if we look back, we may be tempted to go back!

Not only will we forget past failures, hurts, rejections and sins as we lay aside the weights and sins that beset me, but we will also forget past blessings and achievements. While very appreciative, we cannot afford to live on yesterday's manna (Ex. 16:20). We need fresh oil from the throne of God each day (Ps. 92:10).

Paul tells us in this passage that one goal consumed his full time and attention. It was to gain full knowledge of Jesus Christ. He is an example of someone who has the 'one thing.' Learning from Paul, we should not let anything take our eyes off our goal – knowing Christ. With the single-mindedness of an athlete straining toward the finish line, we must lay aside anything that may be in the way of our fellowship with Jesus.

## NOTES

# Charity Morris

# Chapter 7

# Keeping the Main Thing the Main Thing

*Deuteronomy 6:4
Hear, O Israel: The Lord our God,
the Lord is one!*

The Lord is one. God is one. He is not divided into two. He is not six. He is one. This idea of oneness in this particular scripture is referencing the exclusivity, the exceptionality, the distinctiveness of our great God. He is <u>THE</u> one. He is unique in Himself. There is no one who can compare to Him. This is no one who can claim the feats He's done. There is no one who can claim to have created Him. He's God. Before time began, He was there. Before light was, He was there. He is stands head and shoulders above all the gods of this world, above all the things that would claim our time, talent, treasure, devotion and attention. The God of Israel is <u>THE</u> only true and living God.

To get a deeper meaning of the content and a greater understanding of the context, we need to look at the original connotation. The Hebrew word "one" means to unite, so one of the tenses means "united." This is transcribed as 'The Lord your God is united.' A perfect depiction of this united tense can be found in Psalm.

> *Psalm 86:11. Teach me Your way, O Lord; I will walk in Your truth;* **unite** *my heart to fear Your name.*

This prayer is one that is at the core of all that I do for God: *Make my heart one with You*. Make my heart so that it becomes concentrated, singularly focused on **<u>ONE</u>** thing, our great God, so that nothing and no one will disrupt the flow in His presence. Unite my heart to reverentially fear and magnify Your name. Give me a heart that has a single, *clear* image of Your goodness, grace and glory. If the desire is to be of one, unified heart, then there is opportunity to have a divided and distracted heart.

Verse five of Deuteronomy 6 further drives the point of being of one heart.

> Deuteronomy 6:5 – *You shall love the Lord your God with all your heart, with all your soul, and with all your strength.*

We can revisit what we learned about Martha and Mary. Jesus' visit with Martha and Mary is a lesson on the importance of responding to the Lord over the numerous concerns and demands of life. Martha worried herself over many things, Mary was singularly focused on only one. Mary was locked in, with the whole of her attention on the guest of honor, Jesus, and His word. Truth is there are many things that will command our time, care and attention. Jesus is at the helm of the table, reminding us to stay focused on who's in our midst and to not take on the cares of this world over being the presence of the One who can carry our cares. This is the one necessary thing.

It appeared as if Mary's choice made Jesus top priority in her life. Her actions reflected "God is FIRST place in my life!" After all, it sounds like it should be a "good Christian" thing to do right? If God is first place in our life then we are doing the right thing, the needful thing – we are putting Him above all else. He is first, then family, ministry, career, and everything else – sounds correct, right? Wrong! It puts God on a list, and that's insulting to Him!

What is meant by "putting God first place" is that we need to prioritize Bible reading, prayer, and other "spiritual activities" above everything else, because, after all, we are to seek ye first the Kingdom of God, right? The suggestion is that everything else is "worldly" and therefore not as good as the "spiritual" things.

Because Christ is in us, He is with us, joined to us, and present in all aspects of our life. Christ is our life. He does not want to be first place in our life. He is the substance of everything about us and in us.

Instead of religiously trying to keep God first place in our life, I ask that we have Him be intimately involved in EVERY aspect of our life. With that, our "priority list" regarding Christ should look like this:

1. Christ is a part of our life – in worship, prayer, Bible reading, church attendance, volunteerism

Keeping the Main Thing

1. Christ is a part of our life – in our family, in our home

1. Christ is a part of our life – in our careers, on our jobs

1. Christ is a part of our life – in our hobbies and interests

1. Christ is a part of our life – in our parenting, coffee drinking, joking around

1. Christ is a part of our life – in our relationships and friendships

1. Christ is a part of our life – in our choice we make for schools and majors

From the least to the greatest activity, Christ is intertwined and involved in it all. There's no sense in comparing Jesus with other things and ranking Him as number one. He isn't separate from all other activities; He is intimately involved in every part and moment of our life.

Think about it. If we have priority lists, we can get our Jesus fix at the top, check off those boxes and do whatever else we want throughout the day, independent of Jesus' involvement and input. I invite you to transcend from chore to communion. Reading and meditating on the Word is good, but invite Holy Spirit into conversations, into decisions that are to be made. Ask God for His wisdom with this next move that you have to make. Even which route to take for work, ask Him which way to go. This may sound trivial or doing the most, but trust me, when we become developed in getting God involved in *EVERY* aspect of our life, things will work out much better.

As we keep this Christ-centered life, it will help us to remain focused on what's really important, and even greater, a Christ-centered life helps us to remain humble. the enemy of all righteousness is constantly lurking and looking for an opportunity to catch us slipping. satan's first appearance on the biblical scene was with one suggestion, one thought, one temptation: exchange their God-centered lives for lives that focused on themselves. God had given Adam and Eve everything that they could ask for, think or imagine; all things were theirs to freely enjoy, except for one tree. Instead of relishing in all that God had so generously bestowed upon them, Adam and Eve decided to focus their attention on the *wrong one thing!* satan's tactic was to shift their focus from the presence of God to self: *Why must **YOU** not eat of these trees? Why should **YOU** be deprived? God knows **YOU** will be like Him if you eat from it – because **YOU** will then have a knowledge of good and evil.* Adam and Eve, as you know, bit the bait and man forsook God to place **themselves** at the center of their own affections, and immediately, division and self-preservation came. Adam and Eve ran and hid themselves out of shame and embarrassment. Adam blamed Eve and God for giving him Eve. Eve blamed the serpent for tricking her and God for creating the serpent. satan is sitting back laughing and saying **"GOT 'EM!"** God had to remove them from His presence. It's a total debacle. This bitter root of self-centeredness would be passed on to every generation. Paul's passage in Timothy sums it up best:

> *2 Timothy 3:2-4 – For people will be lovers of self, lovers of money, proud, arrogant, abusive, disobedient to their parents, ungrateful, unholy, ³ heartless, unappeasable, slanderous, without self-control, brutal, not loving good, ⁴ treacherous, reckless, swollen with conceit, lovers of pleasure rather than lovers of God.*

As we return back to being unified with and living a Christ-centered life, the struggle to self-protect, self-promote, self-provide will lessen. As we surrender our will for His will, our ways for His way, our plans for His plan and our paths for His path, we will discover a more excellent way, we will see a supernatural way of doing and being and we will begin to operate according to the Kingdom's protocol.

*Deuteronomy 6:4-19 – <sup>4</sup> Attention, Israel! GOD, our God! GOD the one and only!*

*<sup>5</sup> Love GOD, your God, with your whole heart: love him with all that's in you, love him with all you've got!*

*<sup>6-9</sup> Write these commandments that I've given you today on your hearts. Get them inside of you and then get them inside your children. Talk about them wherever you are, sitting at home or walking in the street; talk about them from the time you get up in the morning to when you fall into bed at night. Tie them on your hands and foreheads as a reminder; inscribe them on the doorposts of your homes and on your city gates.*

*<sup>10-12</sup> When GOD, your God, ushers you into the land he promised through your ancestors Abraham, Isaac, and Jacob to give you, you're going to walk into large, bustling cities you didn't build, well-furnished houses you didn't buy, come upon wells you didn't dig, vineyards and olive orchards you didn't plant. When you take it all in and settle down, pleased and content, make sure you don't forget how you got there—GOD brought you out of slavery in Egypt.*

*<sup>13-19</sup> Deeply respect GOD, your God. Serve and worship him exclusively. Back up your promises with his name only. Don't fool around with other gods, the gods of your neighbors, because GOD, your God, who is alive among you is a jealous God.*

## NOTES

Charity Morris

# Prayer of Salvation

A number of years ago in California, fierce winds from a dust storm triggered a massive freeway pileup. At least 14 people died and dozens more were injured as topsoil whipped by 50 mile-per-hour winds reduced visibility to zero. The afternoon disaster left a three-mile trail of burning vehicles, some stacked on top of each other. The problem was, no one was able to see. Many of the motorists blindly drove ahead, right into the disaster. Spiritually, this was each of us and it is you who are not born again. You can't see what you need to see. And unless someone intervenes, you're going to blindly drive your soul right into the disaster of hell, condemned and separated from God for an eternity.

But God, in His infinite wisdom and grace, provided a way of escape for you through Jesus Christ. He came to remove the blindness and restore you to the Father. You may think your past is too much to forgive. Trust me, your past is no match for the power of Jesus' redemptive blood. If He could use flawed individuals like Christ-denying, faithless Peter, murdering Moses, philandering David, and the terrorist

Paul, your situation is not impossible. He can clean you and make you fit for the Master's use in the Kingdom.

If you are ready to join the family of God, simply pray this prayer out loud:

*Lord Jesus, I believe You are the Son of God who died for my sins. I confess with my mouth and believe in my heart that God raised You from the dead. Forgive me of all my sins. Be Lord of my life for the rest of my life. Amen.*

If you prayed that prayer with a sincere heart, you are now saved. Hallelujah! Now it's important for you to find a church home that can help you grow and succeed in your spiritual walk. If you do not know of one, send an email to info@scribepublicationsinc.com and they will connect you with a church in your area.

# Biography

Charity A. Morris, a native of Chicago, IL, is the fourth of six children born to Apostles David and Dorothy Nelson of New Destiny of Faith Ministry in Louisville, KY.

Charity received Christ into her heart in August 1985, at the age of 7. As a child and even today, one of her greatest and strongest spiritual mentors has been her mother, Dorothy, who has been effectively ministering for over 30 years.

Charity is a dynamic teacher of God's Word who has a gifted ability to teach with clarity, simplicity, revelation and power. She has been blessed to travel throughout the U.S., Europe and Africa assisting with mission programs and ministering The Word of God.

She holds a B.A. in Psychology and an A.A. in French from Indiana University Northwest. In 2009, she also graduated from the Joseph Business School, under the leadership of Dr. Bill Winston, Pastor of Living Word Christian Center. Charity's entrepreneurial gifts manifested as she started her own publishing company, Scribe Publications.

Charity's work is her worship. Her heartbeat is seeing people experience the fullness of God. She is passionate about expanding God's Kingdom. Charity is the wife of Elder Gary Morris of Marvelous Light Christian Ministries. Together they have four beautiful children and reside in Georgia.

If you would like to book Charity to speak at your conference, service, or event, please email info@charitymorris.com and we will get back to you within 24 hours.

www.ingramcontent.com/pod-product-compliance
Lightning Source LLC
Chambersburg PA
CBHW020429010526
44118CB00010B/489